Counting
Ladybugs
1-2-3

Brian Enslow

Enslow Elementary
an imprint of
Enslow Publishers, Inc.
40 Industrial Road
Box 398
Berkeley Heights, NJ 07922
USA

http://www.enslow.com

Library of Congress Cataloging-in-Publication Data

Enslow, Brian.
 Counting ladybugs 1-2-3 / Brian Enslow.
   p. cm. — (All about counting bugs 1-2-3)
 Summary: "Learn about bugs, and counting to ten"— Provided by publisher.
 Includes bibliographical references and index.
 ISBN 978-0-7660-3922-3
 1. Ladybugs—Juvenile literature. 2. Counting—Juvenile literature. I. Title. II. Title:
Counting ladybugs one, two, three.
 QL596.C65E57 2012
 513.2'11—dc23   2011014454

Paperback ISBN: 978-1-59845-251-8

Printed in the United States of America

052011 Lake Book Manufacturing, Inc., Melrose Park, IL

10 9 8 7 6 5 4 3 2 1

Cover and Illustration Credits: Ladybugs: Dmytruk Olena/Shutterstock.com;
Cover Background: Oksana Merzlyakova/Shutterstock.com; Ice Cream: abrakadabra/
Shutterstock.com.

Note to Parents and Teachers

Help pre-readers get a jumpstart on reading. These simple texts introduce new concepts
with repetition of words and short simple phrases. Photos and illustrations fill the pages
with color and effectively enhance the text. Free Educator Guides are available for this
series at www.enslow.com. Search for the **All About Counting Bugs 1-2-3** series by name.

Contents

Words to Know

ladybug

one

ten

1

one ladybug

2

two ladybugs

3

three ladybugs

4

four ladybugs

5

five ladybugs

6

six ladybugs

7

seven ladybugs

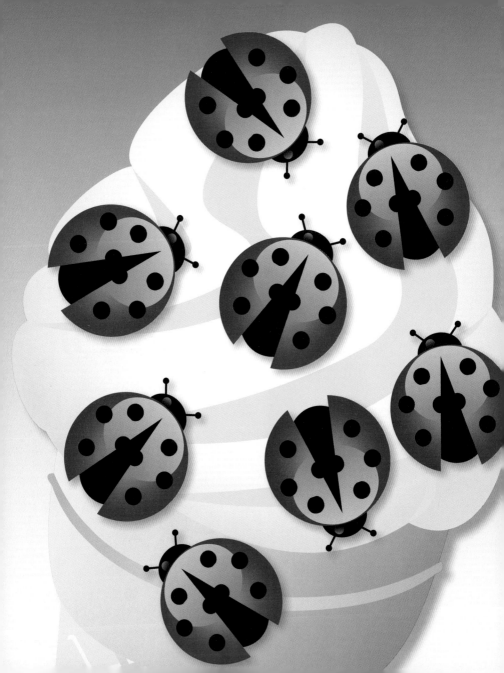

8

eight ladybugs

9

nine ladybugs

10

ten ladybugs

Read More

Dahl, Michael. *Lots of Ladybugs!: Counting by Fives.* Mankato, MN: Picture Window Books. 2004.

Parker, Kim. *Counting in The Garden.* London, UK: Orchard Books. 2005.

Web Sites

Cartoonito
<http://www.cartoonito.co.uk/games/how-many>

Everything About Ladybugs!
<http://everything-ladybug.com/index.php>

Index

Guided Reading Level: **A**
Guided Reading Leveling System is based on the guidelines recommended by Fountas and Pinnell.

Word Count: **20**